Profiles of the Presidents

ZACHARY TAYLOR

★ ★ ★

Profiles of the Presidents

ZACHARY TAYLOR

by Robin S. Doak

Content Adviser: Harry Rubenstein, Curator of Political History Collections, National Museum of American History, Smithsonian Institution

Reading Adviser: Dr. Linda D. Labbo, Department of Reading Education, College of Education, The University of Georgia

COMPASS POINT BOOKS MINNEAPOLIS, MINNESOTA

Compass Point Books
3109 West 50th Street, #115
Minneapolis, MN 55410

Visit Compass Point Books on the Internet at *www.compasspointbooks.com*
or e-mail your request to *custserv@compasspointbooks.com*

Photographs ©: White House Collection, Courtesy White House Historical Association, cover, 1; Hulton/Archive by Getty Images, 6, 8, 10, 13, 17, 19, 22, 29, 34, 36, 37, 39 (all), 40 (all), 44, 48, 49, 50, 54 (all), 55 (right, all), 57 (right), 59; Bettmann/Corbis, 7, 21 (top), 43, 56 (bottom left); North Wind Picture Archives, 9, 11, 16, 20, 25, 28, 30, 46, 47, 56 (top left), 57 (left); Library of Congress, 14, 41, 55 (left); Stock Montage, 15, 24, 31, 32, 35, 58 (bottom left); G.E. Kidder Smith/Corbis, 18; Alabama Department of Archives and History, Montgomery, Alabama, 21 (bottom); Lombard Antiquarian Maps & Prints, 26, 58 (top left); National Portrait Gallery, Smithsonian Institution/Art Resource, N.Y., 27; Department of Rare Books and Special Collections, University of Rochester Library, 56 (bottom right); Bruce Burkhardt/Corbis, 58 (right).

Editors: E. Russell Primm, Emily J. Dolbear, Melissa McDaniel, and Catherine Neitge
Photo Researchers: Svetlana Zhurkina and Heidi Schoof
Photo Selector: Linda S. Koutris
Designer/Page Production: The Design Lab/Les Tranby
Cartographer: XNR Productions, Inc.

Library of Congress Cataloging-in-Publication Data
Doak, Robin S. (Robin Santos), 1963–
  Zachary Taylor / by Robin S. Doak.
     v. cm.— (Profiles of the presidents)
Includes bibliographical references and index.
Contents: A commitment to the Union—Growing up in Kentucky—A young frontier officer—Old Rough and Ready—The Mexican War—The people's president—The end of a fine career—Glossary—Zachary Taylor's life at a glance—Zachary Taylor's life and times—World events—Understanding Zachary Taylor and his presidency.
  ISBN 0-7565-0260-8 (hardcover)
 1. Taylor, Zachary, 1784–1850—Juvenile literature. 2. Presidents—United States—Biography—Juvenile literature. [1. Taylor, Zachary, 1784–1850. 2. Presidents.] I. Title. II. Series.
 E422 .D627 2003
  973.6'3'092—dc21   2002010051

Table of Contents

★ ★ ★

*NOTE: In this book, words that are defined in the glossary are
in* **bold** *the first time they appear in the text.*

A Commitment to the Union

★   ★   ★

Zachary Taylor was a man of courage and principles. For more than forty years, Taylor served his country as an army officer. On the battlefield, he proved his bravery and loyalty to the United States. Later, when Taylor was called upon to lead his nation, he gave the job his all. To Taylor, nothing was more important than the well-being of the United States of America.

Taylor became the twelfth U.S. president at a critical time in U.S. history. The issue of slavery was beginning to rip the nation apart. In time, it would lead to the Civil War (1861–1865) between

Zachary Taylor, ▶ American general and twelfth president of the United States

Slaves picking cotton on a Southern plantation

the Northern and the Southern states. Taylor was a Southerner. He owned slaves, and he supported allowing slavery in the South. He surprised many people, however, by refusing to allow the spread of slavery to the West.

Called "Old Rough and Ready" by his soldiers and admirers, Taylor was up to the challenge of running the country. Whether facing enemy troops or unfriendly politicians, he stood firm. As a soldier, Taylor spent his life fighting for the Union. As president, he found his role no different. He quickly saw that his most important task was to keep the United States together.

Growing Up in Kentucky

★ ★ ★

Zachary Taylor impressed those who met him as a down-to-earth man who came from humble beginnings. Few people would have guessed that Taylor was part of a wealthy and well-respected Virginia family.

Zachary Taylor was born on November 24, 1784, near Barboursville, Virginia. His father, Richard Taylor, and his

Zachary Taylor ▶ was born in this home near Barboursville, Virginia.

mother, Sarah Dabney Strother Taylor, both came from well-to-do Virginia families.

Zachary's father had served in the Revolutionary War (1776–1781) under General George Washington. At the end of the war, Lieutenant Colonel Taylor was given 6,000 acres (2,428 hectares) of land in Kentucky for his service to the new nation. Shortly after Zachary's birth, the Taylors headed across the Appalachian Mountains to their new home.

The move to Kentucky was a good one for Richard Taylor and his family. As the years went on, the Taylors thrived. In time, they moved from their small log cabin

◀ *A settler's log cabin in the Appalachian Mountains*

into a large brick home. As Richard became wealthier, he purchased more land. He also bought more slaves to work the land. By 1810, Zachary's father owned thirty-seven slaves and 10,000 acres (4,047 hectares) of land.

When the Taylors moved to Kentucky, the region was wild. Only a few white settlers lived there. Zachary's father played an important role in Kentucky's growth. Richard gained fame throughout the region for fighting Native Americans. He also held a number of government positions, including justice of the peace and state legislator. President George Washington gave Richard the

Famous ▶
frontiersman Daniel
Boone leading
settlers through the
Kentucky wilderness

important job of collector of customs for Louisville, a thriving port on the Ohio River. This meant that Taylor collected the taxes for the federal government on goods brought up the river.

Zachary Taylor had many brothers and sisters. They spent their childhood learning how to survive in the wilderness. Young Zachary quickly learned how to hunt, fish, ride horses, and help out on the farm.

◀ *Founded in the late 1700s, Louisville had become a thriving city by the mid 1800s.*

Zachary attended a local school for a short time, and he sometimes had tutors. He did not, however, receive the formal education that most other future presidents did. Despite his lack of schooling, Zachary was quick-thinking, intelligent, and fearless.

As a young boy, Zachary listened to his father's stories about George Washington and the Revolutionary War. In Kentucky, he watched his father go off to battle Native Americans. Zachary dreamed that one day he would be the one going off to fight. As he grew older, Zachary Taylor told his family that he wanted to be a soldier.

In 1808, Taylor entered the U.S. Army as a lieutenant. In just two years, he was promoted to the rank of captain and sent to New Orleans, Louisiana.

In 1810, Taylor married Margaret "Peggy" Mackall Smith. Born in 1788, Peggy was the daughter of a wealthy Maryland farmer. She met Taylor in 1809 while she was visiting her sister in Louisville. After their marriage, Peggy moved to a small farm near Louisville. The farm was a wedding present from Taylor's father. In the years to come, Peggy and Zachary Taylor had five daughters and a son.

Growing up, Zachary Taylor heard stories of George Washington (shown here) and the Revolutionary War.

Zachary and Peggy ▸
Taylor's home in
Saint Matthews,
Kentucky

For the forty years she and Zachary were married, Peggy was a devoted and loving wife. Although she was in fragile health, she followed her husband from one fort to another. She often moved to the wildest parts of the country to be closer to him. During their life together, Peggy and Zachary lived in Kentucky, Indiana, Louisiana, Wisconsin, and other places far from the world Peggy knew. Neither of them would have guessed that they would one day make their home in the White House.

A Young Frontier Officer

★ ★ ★

In the early 1800s, pioneers were crossing the Appalachian Mountains by the thousands. They were searching for new homes in the West. Many settled on land that Native American tribes considered their own. The resulting battles between American Indians and white settlers were often violent and bloody.

◀ Native Americans attacking white settlers in their home

Shortly after his marriage, Zachary Taylor was put in charge of Fort Knox in Indiana. This was the first of many assignments that placed Taylor on the front line of the battles between Native Americans and white settlers and traders. Taylor's job was to protect the settlers and traders and to keep the peace on the **frontier.**

Taylor was still in Indiana when the War of 1812 (1812–1814) broke out between the United States and Great Britain. In part, the war was a struggle for control of lands in the American West. Battles raged in these **territories.** Both nations were determined to hold on to the land.

U.S. forces fighting the British at the Battle of New Orleans during the War of 1812

◄ Fort Harrison in 1812

On September 4, 1812, Taylor and fifty soldiers were stationed at Fort Harrison in Indiana. That evening, the fort was surrounded by more than four hundred Native Americans who were fighting on the side of the British. Led by the great Shawnee chief Tecumseh, the group set fire to the fort. They hoped to burn out the soldiers.

Taylor's men fought fiercely. Urged on by their commander, they refused to give up. By the next morning, Taylor and his soldiers had driven away the Indians. News of the triumph spread rapidly across the nation. Taylor was promoted to the rank of major.

When the war was over, Taylor left the army and returned to his farm in Kentucky. He soon became restless, however. By 1816, after just one year on the farm, Major Zachary Taylor was back in uniform.

Taylor's next assignment took him back to Louisiana. There, Taylor and his men built forts and roads. Life in the swampy state was hard. It took a terrible toll on the Taylor family. In 1820, Peggy and the two youngest Taylor daughters became very ill. Peggy survived, but the girls, Octavia and Margaret, did not.

Despite the sad events, the Taylors stayed in Louisiana until 1828. That year, Zachary Taylor was

Taylor supervised the construction of the Pentagon Barracks at Fort Rouge, Louisiana. It was built between 1819 and 1823.

sent to the upper Mississippi River region, in what is now Minnesota, Wisconsin, Iowa, and Illinois. He continued to perform his duties well, and in 1832, he was promoted to colonel.

That April, the Black Hawk War began. The war started when Chief Black Hawk and a group of Sauk and Fox Indians tried to reclaim land in Illinois that the United

▼ *Black Hawk, a chief of the Sauk tribe*

States had taken from them. U.S. troops set out after the Native Americans. They hoped to drive them back to their new home in Iowa. As the war heated up, both Native Americans and white settlers were killed.

Taylor and his men helped end the war. By August 1832, they had driven Black Hawk out of Illinois and into Wisconsin. On August 2,

Taylor's soldiers defeated Black Hawk's people in the Battle of Bad Axe. The battle put an end to fighting between whites and Indians in the region.

After the war, Taylor earned a reputation as a man who dealt fairly with Native Americans. Taylor believed that to keep the peace, American Indians and settlers must stay away from each other. He believed that land-hungry settlers were to blame for many of the problems

The Battle of ▶
Bad Axe

between the two groups. He even asked the government to allow him to burn down the homes of settlers who illegally took Native American lands.

Taylor loved being an army officer, but he didn't want a military life for his children. All three of his surviving daughters, however, married army officers. In 1834, Taylor's daughter Sarah Knox married Lieutenant Jefferson Davis. Years later, Davis played an important role during the Civil War. He served as president of the Confederate States of America, the nation formed by the Southern states that tried to break away from the United States. Taylor's own son, Richard, would one day serve as an officer in the Confederate army.

◀ *Jefferson Davis married Taylor's daughter Sarah Knox. She died of malaria within three months of the wedding.*

◀ *Richard Taylor served in the Confederate army*

Old Rough and Ready

★ ★ ★

In 1837, Zachary Taylor was sent to Florida to command troops during the Second Seminole War (1835–1842). During the war, the Seminole people fought the United States to keep control of their land. Taylor's job was to defeat the Seminoles and prepare them for the journey to their new home in Indian Territory (present-day Oklahoma).

Zachary Taylor on horseback directs a brutal attack against the Seminole. ▼

On December 25, 1837, Taylor and more than one thousand men marched into the Florida swamplands around Lake Okeechobee. They defeated a group of 400 Seminoles. The battle marked the beginning of the end for most of the Seminole people in Florida. The Seminoles realized that it was impossible to keep the United States from taking their land. Many gave up.

The battle against the Seminoles brought Taylor even more fame across the nation. In 1838, he was promoted to the rank of brigadier general. He was in charge of all U.S. forces in Florida. During that time, Taylor got the nickname that would stick with him through the rest of his life: Old Rough and Ready. Taylor's soldiers said that although Taylor dressed roughly, he was always ready for battle. Taylor's bravery and his habit of staying in the thick of the fighting earned him the respect and devotion of his men.

In 1840, Taylor tired of his Florida command. He requested a leave from the army. Through the years, he had bought a number of **plantations**. While he was in the army, Taylor relied on managers to oversee his land. He kept in touch with the managers by mail, sending them long letters filled with instructions and questions.

While he was on leave, Taylor turned his attention to his plantations.

Eventually, Taylor owned plantations in Kentucky, Louisiana, and Mississippi. By the time of his death in 1850, he also owned nearly 150 slaves. Taylor believed that Southern plantations needed slaves to succeed, but he did not favor allowing slavery in parts of the nation without plantation farming. Because of such beliefs,

Slaves working on one of Taylor's plantations

people would later call him "a Southern man with Northern principles."

Taylor never sold any of his slaves. One Christmas, he even gave $500 (a very large sum at the time) to be divided among the slaves on one of his plantations. Taylor felt no guilt about owning other humans, however, and he didn't instruct that any of his slaves should be freed when he died.

◄ *Slaves were bought and sold at auctions.*

In June 1841, Taylor left his plantations to return to the army. He was put in charge of troops in Louisiana, Arkansas, and Oklahoma. Taylor and his men helped keep the peace among the many Native American tribes in the area.

Commander Zachary Taylor in his formal uniform

Although Taylor was a general, he still did not dress formally. Instead of wearing a crisp army uniform, Taylor put on baggy cotton pants and an old jacket. He completed his outfit by wearing a big straw hat to keep the sun off his face. Soldiers got used to seeing the general riding through camp on his trusty horse, Old Whitey. A fellow officer once remarked that Taylor looked like an old farmer on his way to the market.

The first few years after Taylor returned to the army were quiet and uneventful. But in the summer of 1845, things began to change. Tensions were growing between the United States and Mexico, its neighbor to the south.

Settlers who had moved to northern Mexico from the United States had risen up against Mexican rule in the Texas region. They won their independence from

▲ Taylor in his casual style of dress, standing third to the right of Old Whitey

Mexico in 1836. After that, they asked to be part of the United States. In March 1845, Congress agreed to add Texas to the United States. Nine months later, Texas became the twenty-eighth U.S. state. Mexicans were furious. They didn't think that the United States had any right to land that had once been theirs.

Houston, Texas, in the mid 1800s ▼

Nor did the two nations agree on the border between Mexico and Texas. The United States claimed all land north of the Rio Grande. Yet Mexican officials believed that some of this land belonged to Mexico. They said that the Nueces River, near Corpus Christi, Texas, was the border between the two nations.

▲ *President James K. Polk*

As the conflict heated up in 1845, Taylor was ordered to make camp at the mouth of the Nueces River. By September, thousands of soldiers had joined him there. For months, Taylor and his men waited for word from Washington. In early 1846, the message came. President James K. Polk ordered Taylor and his troops to advance to the Rio Grande. Taylor knew that the Mexican army was already there, waiting. If attacked, Taylor and his men were ready to fight.

The Mexican War

★ ★ ★

On March 28, 1846, General Zachary Taylor and four thousand troops arrived at the Rio Grande. Taylor and his men built a fort near the site of what is now Brownsville, Texas. Called Fort Brown, it was across the river from the Mexican town of Matamoros.

In mid-April, a Mexican army commander ordered Taylor to leave the area. Taylor refused. On April 24, Mexican troops crossed the Rio Grande. The Mexicans

General Zachary ▶ Taylor's forces camping on the Rio Grande in 1846

attacked a group of American soldiers who were scouting the area. Sixteen Americans were killed or wounded.

The attack was just what President Polk had been waiting for. He stated that Mexico had invaded U.S. territory and shed American blood. Then he asked Congress to declare war on Mexico. On May 13, 1846, Congress did just that. By then, however, Taylor had already fought the first two battles of the Mexican War (1846–1848).

On May 8, Taylor and his troops were attacked by more than four thousand Mexican soldiers. The attack occurred just north of Fort Brown, at a place called Palo Alto. Although outnumbered, Taylor's two thousand men

◀ *The Battle of Palo Alto*

fought hard. The Americans also had better weapons. The Battle of Palo Alto raged for hours before the Mexicans **retreated.** At the end of the day, five Americans and more than one hundred Mexicans had died.

The following day, Taylor and his men chased the retreating Mexicans. They caught up with them near a dry streambed called Resaca de la Palma. The two sides again fought fiercely. As it became clear that Taylor would win, Mexican soldiers began to flee across the Rio Grande. Many drowned while trying to get to the other side. More than three hundred Mexicans died during the Battle of Resaca de la Palma, while Taylor lost about thirty soldiers.

Taylor's troops ▸ defeated the Mexican army at the Battle of Resaca de la Palma.

The U.S. government awarded Taylor two Congressional Gold Medals for winning the first two battles of the war. He was also promoted to the rank of major general. Then he was ordered to cross the Rio Grande and take control of the city of Matamoros. This proved easy—the Mexicans abandoned Matamoros on May 18.

As news of Taylor's success spread, more men signed up to fight with Old Rough and Ready. The general spent the next two months training his new soldiers. In July 1846, Taylor and more than six thousand troops headed west toward the city of Monterrey. One of Mexico's largest cities, Monterrey was defended by more than seven thousand Mexican troops.

On September 21, Taylor attacked Monterrey. For four days, U.S. troops fought brutal, bloody battles in the city's streets. Throughout the battle, Taylor was right beside his men, urging them to fight fiercely. Taylor's men were inspired by his calmness and bravery. They fought hard, and on September 24, the city fell. The Mexican general **surrendered** to Taylor and asked for an eight-week **truce.** He also asked that he and his soldiers be allowed to take their guns and retreat southward. Taylor agreed.

When President Polk heard about the truce, he was

The Mexican defeat ▲ at Monterrey

furious. He could not believe that Taylor had allowed the Mexican army to escape. Polk ordered Taylor to stop his advance into Mexico. Instead, General Winfield Scott would be given the honor of attacking Mexico City, Mexico's capital. As a final insult, Polk took away half of Taylor's soldiers and sent them to fight with Scott.

Taylor was angry and unhappy about Polk's actions. As always, however, he accepted his orders. He said,

"I will carry out in good faith, while I remain in Mexico, the views of the government, though I may be **sacrificed** in the effort." Taylor moved his remaining soldiers southwest to Agua Nueva, Mexico, to dig in and wait.

▲ General Winfield Scott's troops entering Mexico City

When Mexican general Antonio López de Santa Anna learned about this, he decided that Taylor would be an easy target. Santa Anna and twenty thousand Mexican troops advanced toward Taylor and his men. On February 22,

1847, the two armies faced off. Santa Anna sent messengers to the U.S. side, demanding that Taylor surrender. Taylor answered with his usual bluntness. "Tell him to go to hell," he said.

The next day, the battle began. As bullets whistled past him, Taylor stood firm. From atop Old Whitey, he urged his men on. During the fighting, two bullets pierced Taylor's coat, but neither one wounded him. The fighting raged for two days. Although badly outnumbered, Taylor's

Mexican general ▶
Antonio López de
Santa Anna

troops never gave up. At the end of the battle, it was clear that Taylor had turned almost certain defeat into victory.

Taylor became a national hero. Some people even thought Old Rough and Ready should be the next U.S. president. Soon, Rough and Ready Clubs sprang up throughout the nation. One of these "Taylor-for-President" clubs was founded by an Illinois politician named Abraham Lincoln. Before long, other well-known politicians were saying that they supported Old Rough and Ready, too.

◀ *Abraham Lincoln later became the sixteenth president of the United States.*

The People's President

★ ★ ★

At first, Taylor thought the idea of his running for president was silly. The idea "never entered my head," he said, "nor is it likely to enter the head of any sane person." He told anyone who asked that he was not eager for the job.

Taylor was quick to point out that he had no experience in politics. For more than forty years, he had served the nation as a soldier. He wasn't a member of any political party. In fact, Taylor had never even voted!

In November 1847, Taylor left Mexico and returned to his plantation in Baton Rouge, Louisiana. Over the next few months, support for Taylor spread like wildfire. Finally, the old general made an important decision: If asked, he would run for president. Taylor declared that he was a member of the Whig Party.

In 1847, there were two major political parties in the

United States. One was the Democratic Party. The other was the Whig Party. The Whigs, formed in 1834, had already sent one war hero, William Henry Harrison, to the White House. They were sure that Zachary Taylor would be the second.

◄ *An 1848 election poster for Whig candidate Zachary Taylor*

In June 1848, the Whigs chose Taylor to run for president. Party officials selected Millard Fillmore from New York to run as vice president. Although running as a Whig, Taylor thought of himself as an independent. He promised that if elected, he would be president of all the people.

◄ *Millard Fillmore, Taylor's running mate*

1848 presidential ▶
candidates Lewis
Cass (above)
and Martin
Van Buren

Two other men were also running for president. One was Democrat Lewis Cass of Michigan. Cass believed that settlers in new territories should decide for themselves whether or not to allow slavery. The other was former president Martin Van Buren, who was running as a member of the Free-Soil Party. It had been formed shortly before the election to oppose the spread of slavery into the West. While the Democrats and the Free-Soilers argued over slavery, the Whigs made sure that Taylor kept quiet. People could think what they wanted about him—and they did.

Southerners assumed that Taylor, a slave owner, would support expanding slavery into the new territories. Northerners assumed that Taylor, a career army officer, would do what was best for the Union and prevent the spread of slavery.

On November 7, the country voted. This was the first time that the entire nation had voted together on one day. When the results were in, Taylor had won. On Monday, March 5, 1849, Taylor was sworn in as the twelfth president of the United States. In a speech that day, he promised to work with Congress and "do whatever is right." He also swore to devote himself to the interests of the entire country and to keep the Union whole.

◀ *The inauguration of General Zachary Taylor*

Taylor brought his down-to-earth style into the White House. Visitors were often surprised to see his horse, Old Whitey, grazing on the White House lawn. Some found Taylor spattered with tobacco juice that had dribbled from his mouth. The president was quite proud of his ability to spit tobacco juice accurately from several feet away.

Peggy Taylor stayed away from Washington's social scene. Some people believed that Peggy had made a promise to herself during the Mexican War: If her husband returned alive from the fighting, she would never again go into society. During big White House parties, Peggy usually stayed upstairs in her bedroom. The Taylors' twenty-five-year-old daughter, Mary Elizabeth, acted as hostess instead.

As president, Taylor believed that the government should be run by Congress. Taylor said that he would sign all the bills that Congress sent to him—as long as the bills didn't go against the U.S. **Constitution.** Taylor believed that his job was to preserve the nation. That job would prove to be a difficult one.

◄ Margaret "Peggy"
Smith Taylor

The End of a Fine Career

* * *

By the time Zachary Taylor became president, the issue of slavery threatened to tear the United States apart. The South wanted to keep slavery alive. Many Southerners

An antislavery ▶
meeting in Boston

also wanted slavery in the new territories the United
States had won in the Mexican War. In the North, however, many people wanted to do away with slavery com-
pletely. They were against admitting any new slave territories to the Union.

Although a slave owner himself, Taylor was against
allowing slavery in the new territories. He knew that if
people in California and New Mexico were allowed to
make up their own minds, they would vote to be **Free
States**—states that did not allow slavery. Taylor told leaders in the two territories to create constitutions that

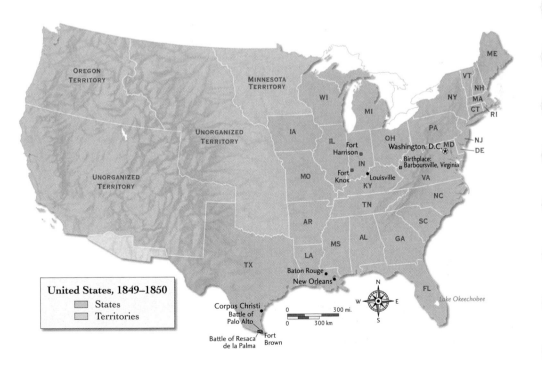

United States, 1849–1850
☐ States
☐ Territories

banned slavery. Then they could ask Congress to be admitted as Free States. This would settle the slavery question without involving Congress at all.

Southern leaders were furious. If California and New Mexico were admitted as Free States, it would upset the balance between slave states and non-slave states in the Union. Some Southern politicians even threatened that their states would leave the Union if slavery was not allowed in California and New Mexico.

San Francisco, ▼ California, around the time politicians were arguing over the issue of slavery in that state and New Mexico

▲ *Santa Fe, New Mexico, in the mid-1800s*

When Taylor heard this, it was his turn to be furious. He bluntly warned Southern leaders that if their states left the Union, he would personally lead the U.S. army against them. Taylor also threatened to hang every traitor to the Union that he could get his hands on.

As the slavery debate heated up, tempers rose in Congress. Fistfights sometimes broke out between politicians. Many even began carrying guns. To keep the peace and protect the Union, some congressmen began working on a **compromise.** They tried to come up with measures that would satisfy both the North and the South.

President Taylor was against any compromise. He would settle for nothing short of California and New Mexico being Free States. Those in favor of compromise would have to wait until after Taylor's death to get their bill through Congress.

During his time in office, Taylor's chief accomplishment was signing the Clayton-Bulwer **Treaty** with Great Britain in 1850. The treaty helped smooth relations between the two countries. Both nations agreed that they would not control any canals built in Central America to link the Atlantic and Pacific Oceans. The treaty also

Kentucky senator Henry Clay (standing) discussing a possible compromise to the debate over slavery

required both countries to stop any efforts to establish **colonies** in Central America. Signing the treaty was one of Taylor's last official acts as president.

On July 4, 1850, Taylor attended a special Independence Day event at the Washington Monument. The day was very hot, and the celebration was long. The president drank glasses of tainted milk and ate fresh fruit. He returned to the White House later in the day with terrible stomach pains.

▼ *Taylor attended a July 4 event at the Washington Monument, which was under construction.*

That evening, Taylor became violently ill. Doctors called to the White House said that he was suffering from food poisoning. The doctors tried to cure the president. Nothing worked.

For five days, Taylor suffered from severe cramps and vomiting. On July 9, he called for his wife. "I am about to die," he said.

"I regret nothing, but am sorry that I am about to leave my friends." Then he died. Taylor had served just sixteen months in office.

Although not a great president, Taylor was remembered as a good man, one devoted to his country. After Taylor's death, journalist Horace Greeley talked about Old Rough and Ready's goodness of heart, his honesty, and his sense of honor. Greeley wrote of Taylor, "A Southern man and a slaveholder, his mind was above the narrow **prejudices** of **district** and class and steadily aimed at the good of the nation as a whole."

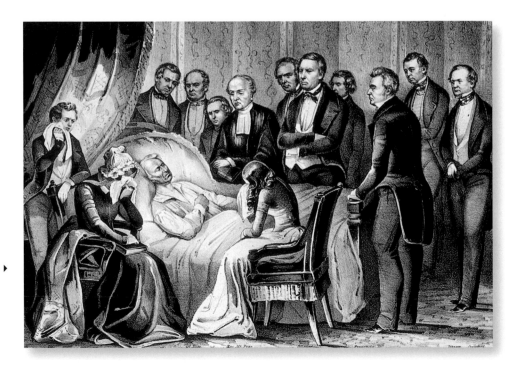

Zachary Taylor ▶ died only sixteen months into his term.

GLOSSARY

★ ★ ★

colonies—territories ruled by people from another country

compromise—an agreement that is reached by both sides giving up part of what they want

Constitution—the document stating the basic laws of the United States

district—region

Free States—states that did not allow slavery in the time before the Civil War

frontier—the edge of settled land in a country

plantations—large farms in the South, usually worked by slaves

prejudices—beliefs that are not based on facts or knowledge

retreated—leaving the battle

sacrificed—lost or given up

surrendered—gave up something important

territories—areas belonging to the United States that are not states

treaty—an agreement between two governments

truce—an agreement to stop fighting in a war

ZACHARY TAYLOR'S LIFE AT A GLANCE

★ ★ ★

PERSONAL

Nickname:	Old Rough and Ready
Born:	November 24, 1784
Birthplace:	Near Barboursville, Virginia
Father's name:	Richard Taylor
Mother's name:	Sarah Dabney Strother Taylor
Education:	No formal education
Wife's name:	Margaret Mackall Smith Taylor (1788–1852)
Married:	June 21, 1810
Children:	Ann Mackall Taylor (1811–1875); Sarah Knox Taylor (1814–1835); Octavia P. Taylor (1816–1820); Margaret Smith Taylor (1819–1820); Mary Elizabeth Taylor (1824–1909); Richard Taylor (1826–1879)
Died:	July 9, 1850, in Washington, D.C.
Buried:	Zachary Taylor National Cemetery near Louisville, Kentucky

PUBLIC

Occupation before presidency:	Soldier
Occupation after presidency:	None
Military service:	Major during the War of 1812; received the surrender of Chief Black Hawk during the Black Hawk War; major general during the Mexican War
Other government positions:	None
Political party:	Whig
Vice president:	Millard Fillmore
Dates in office:	March 5, 1849–July 9, 1850
Presidential opponents:	Lewis Cass (Democrat); Martin Van Buren (Free-Soiler), 1848
Number of votes (Electoral College):	1,360,967 of 2,874,572 (163 of 290), 1848
Writings:	*Letters of Zachary Taylor* (1908)

Zachary Taylor's Cabinet

Secretary of state:
John M. Clayton (1849–1850)

Secretary of the treasury:
William M. Meredith (1849–1850)

Secretary of war:
George W. Crawford (1849–1850)

Attorney general:
Reverdy Johnson (1849–1850)

Postmaster general:
Jacob Collamer (1849–1850)

Secretary of the navy:
William B. Preston (1849–1850)

Secretary of the interior:
Thomas Ewing (1849–1850)

ZACHARY TAYLOR'S LIFE AND TIMES

★ ★ ★

TAYLOR'S LIFE	WORLD EVENTS

1783   American author Washington Irving is born

November 24, Taylor is born near Barboursville, Virginia   **1784**

Family moves to Kentucky   **1785**

1790

1791   Austrian composer Wolfgang Amadeus Mozart (below) dies

1792   The dollar currency is introduced to America

TAYLOR'S LIFE

WORLD EVENTS

1799   Napoléon Bonaparte (below) takes control of France

1800

1807   Robert Fulton's *Clermont* (below) is the first reliable steamship to travel between New York City and Albany

Joins the U.S. Army   1808
as a lieutenant

1809   American poet and short-story writer Edgar Allen Poe is born in Boston

June 21, marries   1810
Margaret Mackall
Smith

Promoted to captain

1810   Bernardo O'Higgins (right) leads Chile in its fight for independence from Spain

TAYLOR'S LIFE

Leads U.S. troops in
the defeat of the
Shawnee chief
Tecumseh during the
War of 1812 (above)

1812

Serves with the army
building forts and
roads in Louisiana

1816

Taylor's wife,
Peggy (below), and
daughters Margaret
and Octavia become
ill; his wife recovers,
but the girls die

1820

WORLD EVENTS

**1812–
1814**

The United
States and
Britain fight the
War of 1812

**1814–
1815**

European states
meet in Vienna,
Austria, to redraw
national borders after
the conclusion of
the Napoleonic Wars

1820

1820

Susan B. Anthony
(below), a leader of the
American woman
suffrage movement,
is born

★

TAYLOR'S LIFE

WORLD EVENTS

1823   Mexico becomes a republic

1826   The first photograph is taken by Joseph Niépce, a French physicist

1827   Modern-day matches are invented by coating the end of a wooden stick with phosphorus

1829   The first practical sewing machine is invented by French tailor Barthélemy Thimonnier (below)

1830

Leads U.S. troops 1832
to victory during
the Black Hawk
War (above)

1836   Texans defeat Mexican troops at San Jacinto after a deadly battle at the Alamo

Commands troops in 1837
Florida during the
Second Seminole War

1837   American banker J. P. Morgan is born

TAYLOR'S LIFE

WORLD EVENTS

Promoted to
brigadier general
1838

1840   1840   Auguste Rodin,
famous sculptor of
The Thinker (below),
is born

Fights the first battles
of the Mexican War
(below)
1846

February 22–23,
becomes a national
hero after winning a
battle against General
Santa Anna during the
Mexican War
1847

1847   The California Gold
Rush begins when
gold is discovered on
the estate of John
Sutter in California

TAYLOR'S LIFE		WORLD EVENTS

Presidential Election Results:	Popular Votes	Electoral Votes
1848 Zachary Taylor	1,360,967	163
Lewis Cass	1,222,342	127
Martin Van Buren	291,263	—

1848 *The Communist Manifesto*, by German writer Karl Marx (below), is widely distributed

Southern states threaten to secede if California enters the Union as a Free State

1849

Signs the Clayton-Bulwer Treaty between Great Britain and the United States, which says that neither nation would control any canals built across Central America

1850 **1850** **1850** California becomes the 31st state admitted to the Union

July 9, dies in the White House

UNDERSTANDING ZACHARY TAYLOR AND HIS PRESIDENCY

★ ★ ★

IN THE LIBRARY

Brunelli, Carol. *Zachary Taylor: Our 12th President.*
Chanhassen, Minn.: The Child's World, 2001.

Deem, James M. *Zachary Taylor.* Springfield, N.J.: Enslow, 2002.

Joseph, Paul. *Zachary Taylor.* Minneapolis: Abdo Publishers, 2000.

ON THE WEB

The American Presidency—Zachary Taylor
http://gi.grolier.com/presidents/nbk/bios/12ptayl.html
For a biography and Taylor's inaugural address

Taylor House
http://www.lhin.lsu.edu/lhin/state_cap/html/taylo.html
For a description and sketches of Taylor's house in Baton Rouge, Louisiana

Zachary Taylor Campaign Poster
http://scriptorium.lib.duke.edu/americavotes/taylor.html
To see a poster from the presidential election of 1848

ZACHARY TAYLOR HISTORIC SITES
ACROSS THE COUNTRY

Fort Jesup State Historic Site
32 Geoghagan Road
Many, LA 71449
318/256-4117
To visit a fort established by
Taylor in 1822

**Fort Zachary Taylor State
Historic Site**
P.O. Box 289
Key West, FL 33041
305/292-6713
To see a fort and a museum
named after the president

**Taylor's Resting Place
The Zachary Taylor
National Cemetery**
4701 Brownsboro Road
Louisville, KY 40207
502/893-3852
To visit Taylor's grave

THE U.S. PRESIDENTS
(Years in Office)

★ ★ ★

1. **George Washington**
   (March 4, 1789-March 3, 1797)
2. **John Adams**
   (March 4, 1797-March 3, 1801)
3. **Thomas Jefferson**
   (March 4, 1801-March 3, 1809)
4. **James Madison**
   (March 4, 1809-March 3, 1817)
5. **James Monroe**
   (March 4, 1817-March 3, 1825)
6. **John Quincy Adams**
   (March 4, 1825-March 3, 1829)
7. **Andrew Jackson**
   (March 4, 1829-March 3, 1837)
8. **Martin Van Buren**
   (March 4, 1837-March 3, 1841)
9. **William Henry Harrison**
   (March 6, 1841-April 4, 1841)
10. **John Tyler**
    (April 6, 1841-March 3, 1845)
11. **James K. Polk**
    (March 4, 1845-March 3, 1849)
12. **Zachary Taylor**
    (March 5, 1849-July 9, 1850)
13. **Millard Fillmore**
    (July 10, 1850-March 3, 1853)
14. **Franklin Pierce**
    (March 4, 1853-March 3, 1857)
15. **James Buchanan**
    (March 4, 1857-March 3, 1861)
16. **Abraham Lincoln**
    (March 4, 1861-April 15, 1865)
17. **Andrew Johnson**
    (April 15, 1865-March 3, 1869)

18. **Ulysses S. Grant**
    (March 4, 1869-March 3, 1877)
19. **Rutherford B. Hayes**
    (March 4, 1877-March 3, 1881)
20. **James Garfield**
    (March 4, 1881-Sept 19, 1881)
21. **Chester Arthur**
    (Sept 20, 1881-March 3, 1885)
22. **Grover Cleveland**
    (March 4, 1885-March 3, 1889)
23. **Benjamin Harrison**
    (March 4, 1889-March 3, 1893)
24. **Grover Cleveland**
    (March 4, 1893-March 3, 1897)
25. **William McKinley**
    (March 4, 1897-
    September 14, 1901)
26. **Theodore Roosevelt**
    (September 14, 1901-
    March 3, 1909)
27. **William Howard Taft**
    (March 4, 1909-March 3, 1913)
28. **Woodrow Wilson**
    (March 4, 1913-March 3, 1921)
29. **Warren G. Harding**
    (March 4, 1921-August 2, 1923)
30. **Calvin Coolidge**
    (August 3, 1923-March 3, 1929)
31. **Herbert Hoover**
    (March 4, 1929-March 3, 1933)
32. **Franklin D. Roosevelt**
    (March 4, 1933-April 12, 1945)

33. **Harry S. Truman**
    (April 12, 1945-
    January 20, 1953)
34. **Dwight D. Eisenhower**
    (January 20, 1953-
    January 20, 1961)
35. **John F. Kennedy**
    (January 20, 1961-
    November 22, 1963)
36. **Lyndon B. Johnson**
    (November 22, 1963-
    January 20, 1969)
37. **Richard M. Nixon**
    (January 20, 1969-
    August 9, 1974)
38. **Gerald R. Ford**
    (August 9, 1974-
    January 20, 1977)
39. **James Earl Carter**
    (January 20, 1977-
    January 20, 1981)
40. **Ronald Reagan**
    (January 20, 1981-
    January 20, 1989)
41. **George H. W. Bush**
    (January 20, 1989-
    January 20, 1993)
42. **William Jefferson Clinton**
    (January 20, 1993-
    January 20, 2001)
43. **George W. Bush**
    (January 20, 2001-)

INDEX

★ ★ ★

ABOUT THE AUTHOR

Robin S. Doak has been writing for children for more than fourteen years. A former editor of *Weekly Reader* and *U*S*Kids* magazine, Ms. Doak has authored fun and educational materials for kids of all ages. Some of her work includes biographies of explorers such as Henry Hudson and John Smith, as well as other titles in this series. Ms. Doak is a past winner of an Educational Press Association of America Distinguished Achievement Award. She lives with her husband and three children in central Connecticut.